# Go To Town

By Najeeb Khan

Illustrated by Mike Dammer

**Target Skill** Letter Recognition *Tt, Uu, Vv, Ww, Xx, Yy, Zz*
**High-Frequency Words** *the, little*

I am the little bus.

LIBRARY

I am the little library.

I am the little school.

MUSIC

I am the little music store.

I am the firefighter.

I am the vet.

Am I happy?